To Juanita —
thanks for your support —
with compliments
Valerie

New York, 1989

Cabbages

&

Geraniums

Memories of the Holocaust

by Valerie Jakober Furth

SOCIAL SCIENCE MONOGRAPHS, BOULDER
DISTRIBUTED BY COLUMBIA UNIVERSITY PRESS, NEW YORK
1989

Contents

Preface

THE HOLOCAUST, the term that has come to mean the Nazi extermination of European Jews, has entered the mainstream of public discourse during the past decade. Survivors have played a central role in this process of understanding the past that is also an essential and inescapable component of the present. Thus, Valerie Furth's memoirs, *Cabbages and Geraniums,* tells us her individual story, as well as the collective account of her family's harrowing odyssey. It is part of the traumatic and tragic fate of Carpatho-Ruthenian and Hungarian Jews during World II.

The unusual title, *Cabbages and Geraniums,* is an explicit reference to Valerie Furth's experiences at Auschwitz-Birkenau: the geraniums bordering the crematoria as well as those standing today on the window sill of her studio in New York, and the field of cabbages where she and her mother spent one harrowing night at Auschwitz. These deceptively simple metaphors serve as mnemonic devices for her story, which is recounted with the same immediacy and intensity that characterizes her art.

Born in 1926 in the town of Munkacs in Carpatho-Ruthenia, then part of Czechoslovakia, Valerie Furth describes her protected childhood in this rural and orthodox Jewish milieu. When Munkacs was incorporated into Hungary after the Nazi occupation of Czechoslovakia in the spring of 1939, the Jews of Munkacs and Carpatho-Ruthenia became immediately vulnerable to the anti-Jewish measures already in effect in Hungary. These curtailed her possibilities for advanced education because of quotas for Jewish schoolchildren and also resulted in the deteriorating economic situation of her family.

Valerie Furth recounts the story of her entire family, including her brother's service in compulsory labor battalions in the Hungarian-

v

occupied parts of the Ukraine. She recalls the concentration and ghettoization of the Jews in Munkacs after Nazi Germany occupied Hungary in March 1944 and the subsequent deportation of more than 36 members of her family to Auschwitz in May 1944. Various attempts at escape had proved abortive.

This combined personal and family story also reveals the group cohesion that enabled many of them to survive five months of incarceration at Auschwitz-Birkenau, brutal labor conditions at Unterluss, and the additional hardships that confronted them at Bergen-Belsen, where they were liberated. The pragmatic and quiet heroism of her story also reflects the particular aspects of the women's experiences in the concentration camps and the reasons for their resiliency and survival as a family group.

Valerie Furth's memoirs are accompanied in this volume by sixty works of art that extend the autobiographical narrative. This documentary art about the Holocaust enhances our understanding of her experiences. It also enables a broader public to share the private memories communicated through her art. These works of art simultaneously document the enormity of the tragedy of the Holocaust and are also an affirmation of life and survival. Her memories and her art demystify the Holocaust by making it concrete and comprehensible. This slender but rich volume links past and present, affirming the fact that the Holocaust also illuminates our contemporary concerns and human values.

Sybil Milton
Ridgewood, New Jersey
April 1988
Author *Art of the Holocaust*

Dedication

I AM DEDICATING THIS MEMOIR to my husband Frank, whose encouragement, help, and love are a continuing source of strength. Without him, I doubt I could have gone down this road.

Yet, at the same time that I thank him, I also ask his forgiveness for stirring up painful memories of his parents and other family members who perished within the Holocaust. Still, I hope that remembering will help his redemption.

Therefore, I am also dedicating this account to his parents, as well as to my parents and to my oldest brother. Edu died on a death march shortly before liberation. His instruction—"Hold on to mother"—guided me throughout the days and nights of Auschwitz.

I am also dedicating this work to my children, Mark and Peter, and to their children. I am so grateful that I was able to give birth to them. Coming as I did out of darkness and ashes, had I not been able to create new life, I'm afraid my own would have seemed meaningless (Illus. 1). My joy in seeing them grow into special people has softened much pain. Like all parents, but maybe more so, I worry about their future. My love will always be with them.

Furthermore, I would like to thank Professor Randolph L. Braham for his support. Without it, I would not have written this book. Marilyn Miller, my editor, also gave me support, as well as editorial guidance.

By sharing some of my experiences, I would also like to reach out to the next generation, to warn them that it can happen again. I hope that they will find the means to prevent a recurrence. So I am asking that they carry my message, by remembering, by bearing witness when I am gone.

Finally, to those who perished and to those who survived. . . .

Illus. 1. "Coming as I did out of darkness and ashes. . . ."

Cabbages and Geraniums

On THE WINDOWSILL of my studio is a small geranium plant. I've had it for, I don't know how many years. It's perfectly ordinary and I pay it no special attention. Sometimes, though, when I lift my eyes from a painting or sculpture I'm doing, I notice it and say to myself, "That's a pretty flower." Then, wondering how I can feel this, I smile and return to work. The smile, composed of too much knowledge, fades from my face.

Naturally, geraniums bloomed in profusion in the window boxes of Munkacs, the town where I was born sixty-one years ago. Like much of Eastern Europe, Munkacs has had a checkered history, control of it passing from one power to another. Until the end of World War I, the region where it is situated, known then as Sub-Carpathian Ruthenia, belonged to the Hungarian part of the Austro-Hungarian Empire. Then, with the creation of the new nation of Czechoslovakia, the town came under its rule. In 1939, following the invasion of Czechoslovakia by the Nazis, the Hungarians regained control.

Munkacs's population in the years before World War II reflected something of this history. Ruthenians, Ukrainians, Germans and Hungarians crowded its cobblestone streets. Of these, about half were Jews.

For a small town, Munkacs was a lively place: an active and vital educational and business center. It boasted five high schools, two academies, and three gymnasia. Yet, despite the bustle, many were poor, and for Jews, life seemed particularly hard.

But poverty did not inhibit our community's liveliness. Though a few considered themselves assimilated, most of Munkacs's Jews were either Orthodox or Hasidic. The groups clashed frequently

1

with the large, though smaller, Zionist faction. Sometimes a Jewish family like mine expressed a variety of religious views. And so it was that grandmother supported the ultra-Orthodox rabbi, father was Orthodox, mother Orthodox, but with Zionist sympathies, and my brother ardently Zionist.

Such diversity could cause problems. For the third grade, mother registered me in the Zionist-oriented Hebrew school. (I had returned home one day from public school with lice in my hair.) Hearing what mother had done, grandma complained to my father. "What will the Rabbi say," she asked indignantly. Everyone knew that it would be nothing good for he strongly opposed the "godless" Zionists. So, much to my sorrow—all my friends went to the Hebrew school—mother enrolled me in the only other private school in town. My new school happened to be Catholic. Certainly, this represented a rather odd solution to the problem of my education. As you can imagine, the period I spent in parochial school was confusing to a young Jewish child. Here I was, surrounded by nuns, the sound of Hail Marys recited before and after each class, ringing strangely in my ears.

Things became more normal two years later when, at the beginning of fifth grade, I switched to the Hungarian junior high school.

Though most Jews in the region had a hard time, our family was an exception. Father owned a lumberyard and a cement factory. We lived in a large, two-story house set back a little from the Latorca River. Here I was born on a February morning, the youngest of four children.

The eldest, Edward or Edu, as we called him, was ten years older than me. Next came my sister Ilona ("Ilu"), who was almost eight years older. My brother Marcel or Moricz followed; a mere four years separated us. Ilu and I shared a room on the second floor. Later, we were promoted or demoted downstairs, a great advantage for our social life, as we could lean out the front window and flirt with the boys passing by. I admired my sister immensely. Practical and quick, she had broad shoulders and good legs. Above all, she possessed a certain style. In those days, she wore tailored suits with little hats.

Of course, as the youngest, I was spoiled, especially by my father. A quiet man with a twinkle in his eyes, on occasion he exhibited quite a temper. Still, except for me, his outbursts inspired no great fear. At noon every day he walked downtown to do business at the bank. Afterwards, he waited on a nearby corner for me to come out of school. We would then proceed to the coffee house where I voraciously devoured all the pastries I desired.

Mother was less indulgent. Blonde-haired, tall and erect, she had a lively but strict manner. Wisely, father and I never hinted at our coffee house rendezvous. From an early age, I sought to win her approval.

Our house was a happy one. Aunts, uncles, and cousins were always visiting. It was nothing to have ten or twelve at dinner. Upstairs, we even had an elegant parlor for company. It was so grand it was hardly ever used. I liked to creep up there and gaze at the beautiful carpets and paintings. Its two brocade armchairs became a favorite hiding place. When mother called to send me on errands, I snuggled against the back of the bigger of the two chairs, a half-read book in my hands.

Father's lumberyard stretched behind the house. It made a fine playground for my best friend Edith and me. That she was Aryan and I Jewish seemed to make no difference to either of us. Hungarian aristocrats, Edith's family had seen better days, and my father, the owner of the house where they lived, permitted the Achatzs to stay there rent free. Engrossed in our childish games, Edith and I swore that the lumberyard was superior to any playground.

So far, then, my childhood was brightly colored. Yet anti-Semitism remained a fact of life. Sometimes in the streets of Munkacs I heard peasants refer contemptuously to the "dirty Jews." Inside our own house, a Czech IRS inspector once flung open the doors of a glass cabinet containing the family prayer books. Ostensibly searching for documents indicating illegal withholding on my father's part, the man threw the entire contents of the cabinet on the floor. After three days of this petty harassment, father bribed him and he left.

In addition, our parents constantly warned us about anti-Semitism. As a result, even though I had really only indirectly experienced prejudice, I still felt its presence. At this early stage of my life, however, it had little effect on me. Like good thick planks of wood, father's wealth and respectability protected us. (One sign of our family's status was the little pot of change. Either on Tuesday or Thursday, one of the children presided over the pot, dipping into it for coins, which we gave to the beggars who came to our door.)

1938. I now attended Junior High School and had other concerns. During my first year I had gone with my classmates to an air show in a field outside of town. On our way back we passed some older boys from the Zionist school. One of them followed me and asked me for a date. At my age, I wasn't permitted to go out with boys. Undeterred by this obstacle, my admirer began to wait outside my school to walk me home.

We went together for nearly four years. We held hands in the movies. Once in a while we met in the park across the river. All of this was quite exciting because my parents had to be kept in the dark. Considering the size of Munkacs and the number of my relatives living in it, I am astonished that we went undiscovered for as long as we did. After three and one-half years, the inevitable reckoning came. Strolling on the bridge by our house, we bumped into father. Seeing that my friend wasn't wearing a cap, father understood immediately that he attended the Zionist school, a fact that made our alliance doubly objectionable. Nevertheless, even though my parents disapproved, we continued going together.

Meanwhile, outside of Munkacs the clouds gathered and began to move in our direction.

In 1938 in Munich, Adolf Hitler met the leaders of the Western democracies of Europe. To "insure peace in our time," they agreed to let Hitler take over part of Czechoslovakia. Only months later the rest of that unfortunate country fell to the Nazis. For the moment Karpatho-Ruthenia was spared. Hitler consented to the region's acquisition by his Hungarian ally in March 1939.

We greeted the news of this change of our nationhood calmly. Culturally, we had always thought of ourselves as Hungarians. Father had served in the Austro-Hungarian Army during the First World War. My parents spoke both Hungarian and Yiddish, and we children spoke Hungarian and German. (For a while, I even had several German governesses, one of whom I hated with a passion.) Moreover, because of father's position, we had powerful Hungarian friends. In short, though the new government was sympathetic to the Nazis, we felt safe.

And, for the time being, life continued for me in much the old carefree way. But soon more drastic changes began, and even I had to look up and take notice.

One change pained me exceedingly. Shortly after the Hungarians gained control of Munkacs my friendship with Edith had cooled. I faced the reason squarely. Now that her people had gained power, a Jew was no longer "good enough" to be a friend. The days of the lumberyard playground had ended.

Other changes affected us all. On September 1, 1939, Hitler invaded Poland. The first Jewish refugees, some of whom included officers in the Polish army, began to trickle into Munkacs. Like a number of others, my family hid and fed many of these refugees until the Zionist underground smuggled them out of the country (usually to Palestine).

Even I had a part in the drama; I had to play downstairs, pretending nothing unusual was going on, all the while knowing that, upstairs, we had hidden twelve people. My participation did not end there. I volunteered to take food to a poor family that was also hiding refugees. The family lived in another part of town, and during the half-hour trip back and forth I felt myself to be a daring young woman indeed. I had another reason to be secretly pleased. Mother had been proud of me for volunteering. Since she rarely praised me, or not as much as I desired, that she was proud put wings on my feet (Illus. 2).

From the refugees we heard eyewitness accounts of the devastation the war had brought as well as about the persecution of Jews. One woman described some kind of ghetto (the Warsaw Ghetto) where people went without food. She said that they were so hungry that they ate potato peels. Such behavior appeared inconceivable to a protected twelve-year-old, and I confided to my mother that the woman was surely crazy.

It was during this time too that my father was arrested. The authorities held him in custody for three days. After one of his prominent Hungarian friends intervened, he was released. We never did learn the charges against him.

Illus. 2. "That she was proud, put wings on my feet."

Both these experiences caused my parents to change their attitude. For the first time really, they began to be afraid. In their conversation, they used a new word "emigration." In fact, my oldest brother had already started to work with the Zionist underground, which was sending lots of young people to Palestine.

Two years later, when I was fourteen, the entire family of Dr. Sternbach, the noted physician, left for Palestine. Their departure made a tremendous impression on everyone. I remember wanting to go, but my parents wouldn't let me. Even at this late date (it was 1942) my father was still such an established, well-to-do man, that, though he talked of it, I don't think he ever really considered emigration. Not only was he personally secure, but, like most Jews around him, he refused to believe that what happened in Poland could ever happen in Hungary.

By this time I had graduated with honors from Junior High School. This should have been sufficient to insure my acceptance into the secondary school system, but it wasn't. A quota system barred my way. Since the Jews comprised only six percent of the entire population of Hungary, only that percentage was permitted to continue its higher education. I remember well the Latin term of the law that prevented me from continuing in the Hungarian schools: *Numerus Clausus*. The Latin words simply disguised what we all knew was discriminatory practice. Still, things were not absolutely rigidified yet. My Hebrew teacher conducted Jewish classes in the public schools and he had connections. He said that they would admit me to the academy—for a price (about $200, a substantial sum in those days). I waxed indignant. "I'm not going if you have to pay for it," I swore.

The matter was settled differently and satisfactorily: I went to the private Hebrew gymnasium. There, until 1944, I enjoyed a relatively normal adolescence. I was happy and unhappy. By this time I was seeing other boys. School bored me. I dreamed of a glorious future. I saw myself dancing on a stage before a widely applauding audience. I saw my art exhibited in great museums. I saw the lovely costumes I would design for elegant actresses with throbbing voices. Despite the suffering of Jews elsewhere in Europe, I still dreamed and all my dreams were rosy.

The clouds drew closer. In 1942 the government inducted Edu into the military-related labor service system. He was married by then and had a one-year-old child. Father tried desperately to use his influence to get Edu out. He failed and my brother was sent to the Ukraine.

The Hungarian army ran the labor service. Those the army considered unreliable or unfit to bear arms, were placed in the service. (Jews were by definition unreliable.) The labor servicemen were employed in the construction and maintenance of roads, building of fortifications, clearing of mines and other military-related projects for both the Hungarian and the German armies. Working conditions were so bad—the climate harsh, the labor arduous, the food barely edible—that many perished. Uncertainty about Edu's fate hung over us, for after a few letters written in the beginning of his service, we received nothing. Only shortly before he returned a year-and-a-half later did we have any indication that he was alive. Our respite was pitifully brief.

March 19, 1944. Hitler invaded Hungary. The assault abruptly ended the dreams of an eighteen-year-old girl. Within two weeks we wore the Yellow Star. We submitted to a six o'clock curfew. Within less than four weeks we were ordered out of our home and resettled in a two or three block area that had been set aside for Jews. The ghetto I had imagined to be the creation of a crazy woman had travelled to Munkacs. It was to be my new home.

We had left our most valued possessions behind us. On realizing we had to go away, father had one of his trusted workers from the factory dig a bunker in our basement. The man took three days to complete it. During this time we and our relatives accumulated the things we couldn't take with us. Then, like an Egyptian tomb, we filled the newly dug hole with furs, silver, fine linens, objects d'art, and solemnly as mourners, watched father's man seal it.

The hour of our departure came. We had our last dinner at home. It was the second night of Passover. Before dinner, we closed the shutters. That night we ate chicken paprikash. Mother remarked, "The paprikash came out especially well tonight."

The next morning on foot we followed the wagon containing the possessions we had decided to take with us. In misty-gray light we crossed the bridge to the other side of town. Once inside the ghetto we found refuge with an aunt. She simply happened to live within the designated area. Ten of us huddled in one room. The chattering of the women kept me up. "What does it all mean?" "Are we going to stay here?" "If not, where are they taking us? Where? Where?" (Illus. 3)

Illus. 3. "Where are they taking us? Where? Where?"

Outside in the yard, not only sounds but smells assaulted me. The odor of cooking food mixed with that of strong soap. And then from both inside and out came the smell of bodies, of many people living close together.

Nearly all of Munkacs's 15,000 Jews had been herded into the ghetto. We were terrified. Like others, we tried to escape. A group of Jewish boys worked feverishly to forge identity papers. Father obtained one for each remaining member of the immediate family. (Our numbers had been depleted because immediately before we were interned, my sister and her future husband had managed to flee. Although we didn't know it then, they had made it safely to Budapest.) Now, through my father's efforts, my middle brother made it out of the ghetto. One of father's former employees, a Christian naturally, accompanied Moricz on the train that left Munkacs for Budapest. The two passed the inspection point, and half-way to the capital, the other man left my brother and returned to Munkacs. In Budapest my brother found work in a lumber yard. He stayed in the city until July, when life became so perilous that he went to the Swiss consultate and asked for a pass out of the country. The consul gave him a pass to Rumania. Since Rumania was closer to Russia and already partially liberated, it was considerably safer. My brother arrived safely in Bucharest and remained there for the duration of the war.

Edu and his family also tried to escape from the ghetto. The night before their scheduled attempt, Charlotte, his wife, had been up all night throwing up. So Edu decided against boarding the truck that may have carried them to safety.

And what of me? One attempt to get me to safety had already failed. Before we entered the ghetto, my father had begged Edith's family to hide me. The Achatzs refused. (Later we learned that the family had looted our Persian carpets. The only Christian, besides the worker who had accompanied Moricz, remaining loyal was our Ruthenian maid, Paula. She risked her life to bring us food in the ghetto.)

A second attempt to save me was now arranged. Along with a girlfriend, I was to be picked up by a truck. At the last moment my friend changed her mind. She wouldn't leave without the man she loved. And I, in my turn, refused to go without her. My love-struck friend paid with her life for her fidelity. She was to die in Auschwitz.

Because of these circumstances, with nearly 15,000 others, I waited for what would come next. After two weeks, they informed us that we were being relocated to a place where we would be put to work.

When the order to move came, we reacted very quickly. We had no time to prepare ourselves or to think about our situation. We were each permitted to take a knapsack with us. In it we put our immediate necessities—extra underwear, a toothbrush, soap, sweaters, hard salami, sweets. The knapsack also contained items of other value. I remember staying up half the night sewing the ten dollar bills father gave me into its straps. The linings of our coats received other valuables such as gold rings and chains. Everyone had a hidden cache, even my eighty-two-year-old grandmother.

The sun was shining the day we left the ghetto. The dust rose in the road as our grave procession filed into the brick factory near the railroad tracks on the outskirts of town. Along the road, people who had lived beside us for decades watched, most of them silently, some, however, egged the gendarmes on. We stayed in the factory for perhaps three days. My memory of this time is a confusion of sight and sound: strewn knapsacks, cockfeathered Hungarian gendarmes with whips, dogs growling, shouts that rent the air.

Finally, we were herded into a cattle car. In front of me, the gendarmes carried one of my teachers, crippled, into the car. Blood from a beating caked his clothing and face.

We had no idea that we were going to a concentration camp, let alone extermination camp. No rumors had reached us either at home or in the ghetto about mass exterminations. Had I known, I am sure I never would have boarded the train.

The journey seemed endless (Illus. 4). So many bodies pressed together, for about 100 people were crammed into the car. In the suffocating air we smelled our own overwhelming fear and panic. We didn't even have room to lean. Close by me stood my grandmother. Nearly blind, she never complained. She prayed.

I remember the black roughness of the car's walls. I remember the tiny rectangular opening, that hint of a window, through which thimblefulls of air filtered in. I was so hungry, but we had decided to ration our bits of cocoa, our pieces of molasses. I was so thirsty, but we had nothing to drink. I remember darkness, grayness. I remember haze. I remember that, through it all, we still hoped we were going to be resettled for work!

Illus. 4. "The journey seemed endless."

*   *   *

I am sitting in my apartment trying to remember what I least want to remember: Auschwitz. Golden light reflects off the river— for again I live on water, this time it is the East River in New York— flows through the windows until the apartment is filled with it. Around me are the paintings I love, some by me, some by others, and I see, as if for the first time, the electric blues, the sunny oranges, the sportive greens, the plush reds and ochres that I choose to surround myself with. For I love color: bold, rich, vibrating. And now Auschwitz comes to me again, swims toward me in a hazy mist: all grays, blacks, all dullness, the negation of life, swims toward me like the thin soup they gave us to drink. All grayness except for the cabbages and the geraniums.

After what must have been three days in the cattle car, we arrived at Auschwitz (Illus. 5). Somehow, we had all survived the journey. In the first moments, only my brother seemed to recognize what awaited us. He acted quickly, motivated by a concern for each. To me he said, "Hold on to mother, I'll hold onto father." Next he grabbed father and instructed him, "Show him the calluses on your hands and tell them that you are a carpenter." To me, he repeated, "Hold on to mother. Don't let them separate you." Then, he took his 3-year-old son from Charlotte and put him in the arms of her mother. At the moment I only saw what he did, lift the boy from one woman and transfer him to another. A simple act. Only later did its significance register. He had handed his son over so that Charlotte might live. (In the concentration camps, women with babies were gassed immediately. My frail sister-in-law did survive the camps. But neither her husband, mother, or child did.)

Illus. 5. "We arrived at Auschwitz."

The guards intervened, pulled us apart, put the men and women on separate lines. This was the last time I saw Edu alive. The line mother and I were on kept moving. In the front stood a handsome, dark-haired man. I quickly learned that he was Dr. Mengele, the ruler of our prison. It was his custom to preside over the fate of the new arrivals. (The prisoners called him "the Angel of Death.") The procedure we were to learn was simple: to the right, life and work; to the left, extermination (Illus. 6). When we reached the front, I held onto mother tightly. Luckily, though she was in her mid-fifties, she had preserved a youthful appearance, her hair still blonde, her body tall and full. When our turn came, I dragged her with me—to the right. At nearly the same instant, I saw my little nephew, his arms wound around his maternal grandmother's neck, go—to the left. My grandmother and several of my aunts also went to the left.

We, who had survived our first selection and did not know it, continued to a large room. In it, we undressed, had our heads shaved, and moved toward the showers. Seeing the shaved head of one of my English teachers, a small feisty woman, I started to laugh. She came up and slapped me across the cheek. That brought me back to my senses in a hurry. In a second I realized that I was as bald as she. Finally, we were given new clothes—that is, new rags, and sent to a barracks.

Barracks 26, Camp C, consisted of one room roughly the size of a small warehouse. About 1,200 women inhabited this space, 600 on one side of it, 600 on the other. Twelve of our relatives had been put in the same barracks. Besides my mother, I had as companions, my aunt Fannie and her three daughters, who were 18, 22, and 25, four of my other cousins, who were between the ages of 28 and 20, my 25-year-old sister-in-law and her younger sister, who was 22, as well as two other cousins, 21 and 18 respectively. Not only was I with my family, but most of them were my peers.

I am convinced I would not have survived without this intimate group. We gave each other emotional and moral support. We made important decisions as a group. My cousin Nellie, a few years older than me, emerged as our leader. More than once her level-headedness saw us through. Out of our group of fourteen, twelve of us managed to survive.

Illus. 6. "To the right—life and work, to the left—extermination."

First we had to survive the food. The capo—the barracks leader— Polish Jew, supervised its distribution. Her assistants handed each of us a slice from something that looked like a black brick. We took one look and shoved the object into the stove. By the third day we dug out our portions from their hiding place. By then we were so hungry we would have eaten real bricks. We cried at the thought of how we had rationed our precious bits of chocolate and cocoa on the train. Naturally, our knapsacks had been confiscated on our arrival. Some fat-faced SS guard was probably biting into our sweets at that very moment.

Virtually the same sequence was enacted for our only other "nourishment," the dark liquid that passed for soup. On the first day we threw away the slop. By the third day, we gulped it down, even biting into the few slivers of potato floating on its surface and the grains of sand that lay at the bottom.

Shortly after we arrived, the guards handed us some picture postcards. They looked so innocent, these cards. "Write that you're in a working camp and that you're going to do real work here," the guards instructed. We wrote these lies down and mailed the cards to an aunt in another town. These were the so-called Waldsee (a fictitious place) postcards designed to mislead the Jews still awaiting deportation.

Life in Barracks C assumed a routine. Twice a day, in the middle of the night and during the late afternoon, we stood five in a row for "Zähl-Appell" or rollcall (Illus. 7). The middle of night Zähl-Appell was horrible. Rough shouts and the barking of dogs pierced our dreams. We stumbled out of the bunk in the icy dark. The SS

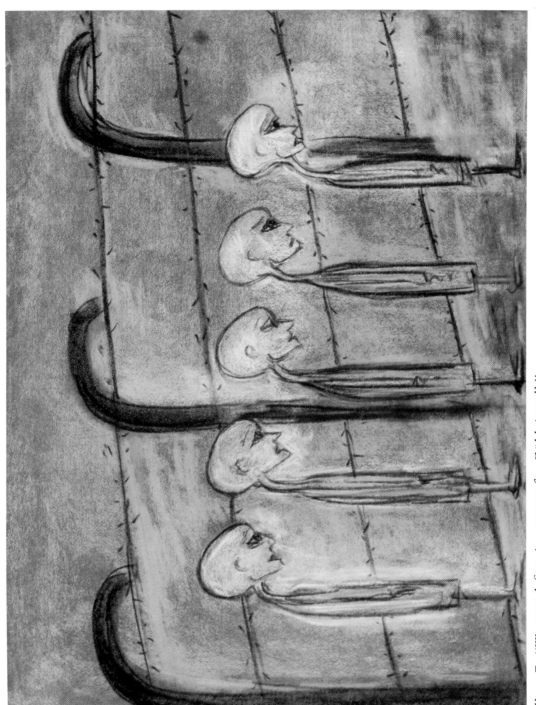

Illus. 7. "We stood five in a row for Zähl-Appell."

let us stand for several hours before beginning the count. Often Zähl-Appell took five hours. During this time, they refused to let us move, though our bowels rumbled and hunger gnawed at our stomachs (Illus. 8).

Once up, our daily work consisted of standing in line for the latrine and keeping ourselves clean. Formidable obstacles stood in the way of these tasks. One latrine served 20,000 women. Most of the time we stood there the entire day. The washroom was next to the latrine. Water flowed from its faucets twice a day. Often we had to fight our way inside. Since my mother had always been personally fastidious, she insisted that I clean myself everyday. Sometimes she even dragged me in herself.

Illus. 8. ". . . our bowels rumbled and hunger knaved at our stomachs."

The rest of the day and the night we sat or lay on our wooden slats looking across the space at one another. We seemed like targets in a shooting gallery—rows of emaciated faces, large staring eyes, the same shaved heads. Time passed in a kind of numbed sameness (Illus. 9 and 10). Our real daily bread was anxiety: would we get through the next twenty-four hours? Our real daily drink was fantasy: mother, for instance, planned menus and cooked the meals in her head. We also fantasized about when and to where we would be liberated. Fervently, I prayed it would be somewhere warm and cosy, for in addition to everything else, we were terribly cold. Lying on our slats, mother and I huddled together, passing whatever warmth we each had into each other. So tightly pressed were we all, that when someone turned, it rippled like a wave through the entire row, as everyone refitted their bodies into the infinitesimal space on earth that had been allotted to them.

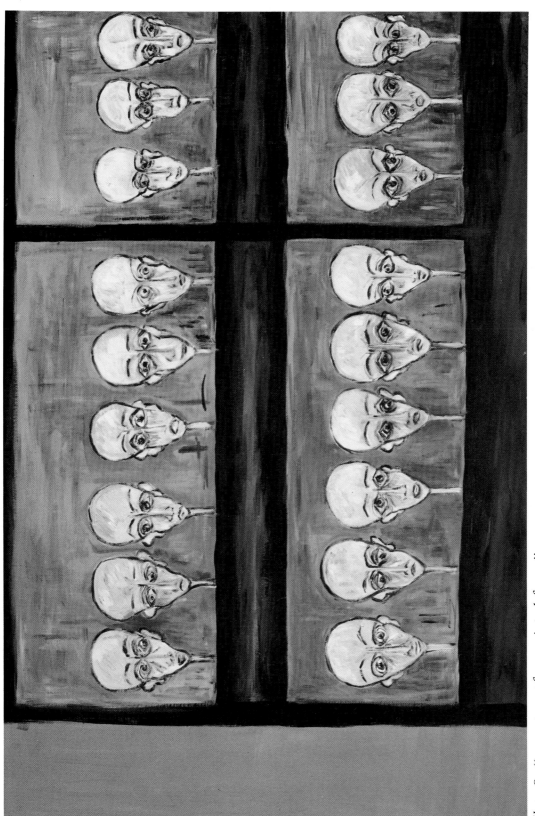

Illus. 9. "... rows of emaciated faces."

Illus. 10. "We seemed like targets in a shooting gallery. . . ."

In reality, Camp C functioned as a way station between transit and the gas chambers. So we waited, and still, miraculously, hoped. While we waited we grew skinnier and skinnier. Our breasts shrivelled like decaying pears. Our legs hobbled about like sticks, and our bones ached, crying for nourishment.

One day the guards marched our block to a group of neat little buildings that appeared to be bathhouses. Bright red geraniums ringed them (Illus. 11). By this time their innocent appearance hardly deceived us. We knew that before us stood the crematoria. Even the geraniums refused to disguise the black smoke, the smell

Illus. 11. "Bright red geraniums ringed them. . . ."

of human flesh that smothered the air around the bathhouses (Illus. 12 and 13). We knew what would happen to us inside those cosy structures. However, it was not our moment to die. Instead, several hours passed while we waited inside of a kind of stall for horses. We waited, not for rescue, but for the end. Finally, using their whips, the guards turned us around like a herd of horses and drove us into a field where cabbages were growing. During the confusion, one guard hit me with his fist and broke my front tooth. We lay down

Illus. 12. "Even the geraniums refused
to disguise the black smoke. . . ."

0

Illus. 13. " . . . the smell of human flesh. . . ."

in the rows between the plants, lay down as if we were to be mowed or dug into the earth itself. Above us, the moon hung like a silver ball in the sky. For some reason, that night it gave off an extremely bright light. Fed by the moonlight, planted in the dark, damp, cold earth, I felt as if I had been resurrected. The next morning our guards marched us back to camp. Yes, I was still alive. Yet why did it seem as though I had left part of myself in that shallow grave in the cabbage field? (Illus. 14, 15, 16, 17, 18, and 19)

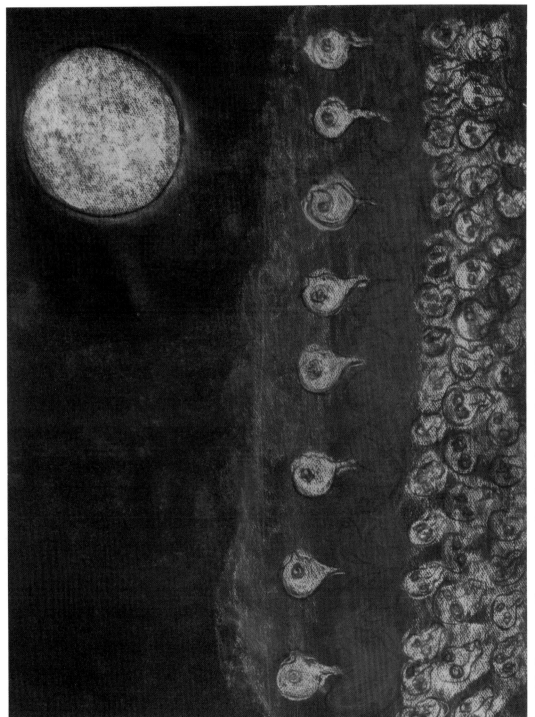

Illus. 14. ". . . as if we were dug into the earth itself."

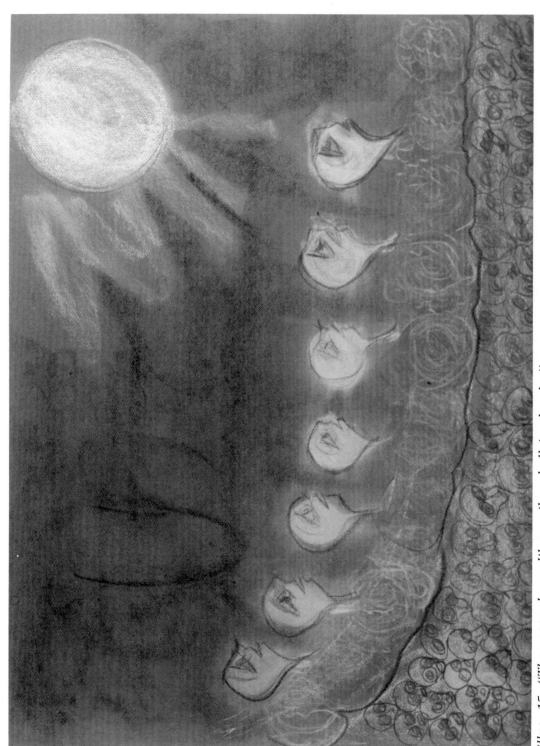

Illus. 15. "The moon hung like a silver ball in the sky."

Illus. 16. ". . . planted in the damp, cold earth, I felt as if I had been resurrected."

38

Illus. 17. "Yes, I was still alive."

Illus. 18. "Yet, why did it seem that I had left part of myself . . ."

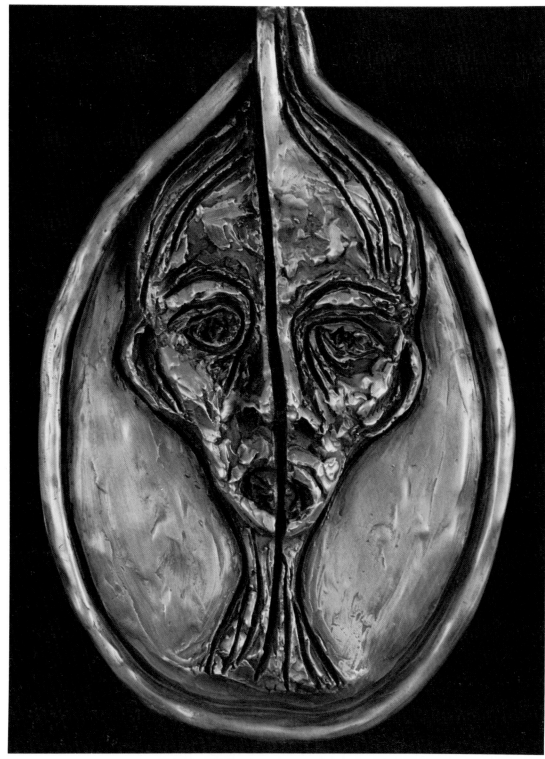

Illus. 19. ". . . in the cabbage field?"

Soon after, during another selection, mother was taken away. She had started to show her age, always a dangerous thing to do, as the Nazis quickly disposed of such muselmänner—or moving mummies as these unfortunates were called. As my mother's back disappeared from sight, I knew with certainty that she was being taken to the crematoria. I begged the capo to let me be part of the day's kitchen brigade. (The capo always selected four or five other prisoners to help her carry back the daily ration.) This way perhaps I could catch one last glimpse of my mother. The capo nodded her head, yes. As we neared the kitchen, I spotted my mother in the midst of the 300 that had been selected. They had not yet been led to the ovens and stood motionless inside the barbed wire (Illus. 20, 21, and 22). Only one guard watched over the group from a lookout

Illus. 20. ". . . and stood motionless. . . ."

Illus. 21. "They had not yet been led to the ovens. . . ."

Illus. 22. "Inside the barbed wire. . . ."

tower. About 100 yards separated me from my mother. I don't know how I had the courage. I broke away from the kitchen detail and ran over to her. She was standing with a glazed look in her eyes (Illus. 23). Seeing me, her eyes cleared. "Oh good," she cried joyfully. "You're here. We will go together."

"Yes," I said. "But let's go back where the others are. We don't know where this group is going."

I grabbed her hand, tugging her away from the group. Like an obedient child she followed me without the slightest resistance. Together, we ran back to our barracks, back to life.

Of that group, only my mother was saved. The mother of a woman in my barracks had also been selected. She never returned. The daughter always reproached me for not having saved her mother too.

Illus. 23. "She was standing, with a glazed look in her eyes."

Choices like mine were made often in a matter of seconds. Yet, all the strands of our lives lead up to them. For me, keeping my mother alive was my most important task at Auschwitz (Illus. 24). Perhaps, it was because she had been more critical of me than my father. Here in camp, I saw how lavishly my aunt praised her daughters. I longed for mother to speak of me in such a way, her spoiled daughter, the lazy girl with a head full of charming dreams, her mouth stuffed in that other, faraway life, with sweets.

(Because of our experience in Auschwitz, our relationship did change. Quite simply, mother became my closest friend. Later, we felt as if we were members of a secret society. The terrifying initiation rights had tested the nature of our attachment, had stripped away the surface and the layer below, and what we saw finally was love. Referring to the times before our internment, mother said to me, "I gave you the least, but I got from you the most." In the end, I too got from her the most, the love I had always craved.)

Illus. 24. "For me, keeping my mother alive was my most important task."

The second time I saw Dr. Mengele, two SS women accompanied him. It was August 1944. We had been in Auschwitz almost four months. Mengele's presence was required for it was another selection. An informant had told us in advance of the selection. She didn't know if the selected would be sent to work in Germany, or used in medical laboratory experiments, or as prostitutes for the soldiers. Whatever happened, it would be better than remaining in Camp C, she advised. Our group met and decided to submit to the selection. Though mother and I were absolutely terrified of selection, we wanted to stay with our relatives. So on the day of selection we remained with the others in the barracks. If we were lucky, we would be sent to a work camp where conditions were somewhat better. If we were unlucky. . . .

Once again we stood before the handsome doctor. Once more we took off all our clothes. The able looking he sent back to the barracks. The others, the Muselmänner he put to one side. While we waited our turn, I watched as the SS women marked the Muselmänner with red x's over their chests (Illus. 25 and 26). We were next. Mengele was momentarily distracted. Mother stood in front of me—by now she looked very emaciated—and when he glanced away, I pushed her into the barracks. Luck was again with us, and we were unobserved.

Illus. 25. ". . . to the Muselmänner, be put to one side."

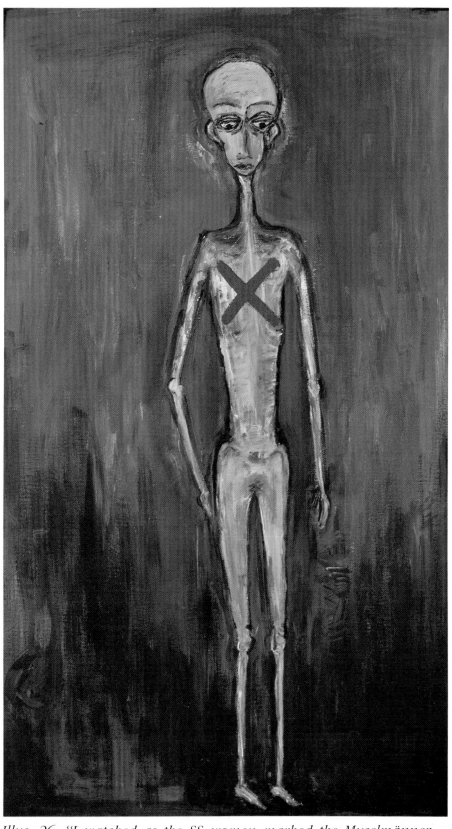

*Illus. 26. "I watched as the SS women marked the Muselmänner
with red X's over their chests."*

We breathed a sigh of relief. Too soon, I'm afraid, for our ordeal had just begun. Our guards led us away. They said we were going to get another shower, before being sent on. Again, the bathhouses with their border of geraniums came into view. Each of us thought, "It's my turn now." Nobody panicked. We stood there quietly. I think we were numb, our limbs unable to move. All we did was to hold on to each other. We stepped inside. The spiggots were turned on and water, real water, streamed down over our bodies (Illus. 27).

Illus. 27. ". . . water, water streamed down our bodies."

After the shower, they gave us some clothes and herded us to the railroad tracks. As we stood by them, a sudden downpour drenched us. Shivering, famished, we waited all night for the trains. When, by morning, they had not arrived, we had to undress again. The SS guards marched us to another barrack in a different camp. For an instant when we entered, we thought they had put us inside an insane asylum. The muddy room was filled with entirely naked creatures. Then we realized we looked exactly like them (Illus. 28).

Illus. 28. "We realized we looked exactly like them."

In that awful room, an intense struggle began. Cold and hunger penetrated our bodies like sharp knives, yet somehow I had to keep my mother's spirit and mine alive (Illus. 29). Looking about me, I vowed we would not become dead souls (Illus. 30).

Two or three days passed like this. Suddenly, a voice on the loudspeaker pierced our numbness. The voice said that "the 800 women selected from Camp C should come to the tracks." From everywhere people started to run. (Thousands of women, seemingly, and all running.) The entire camp was trying to get on the cattle cars. In the tremendous pushing and shoving, I lost hold of my mother.

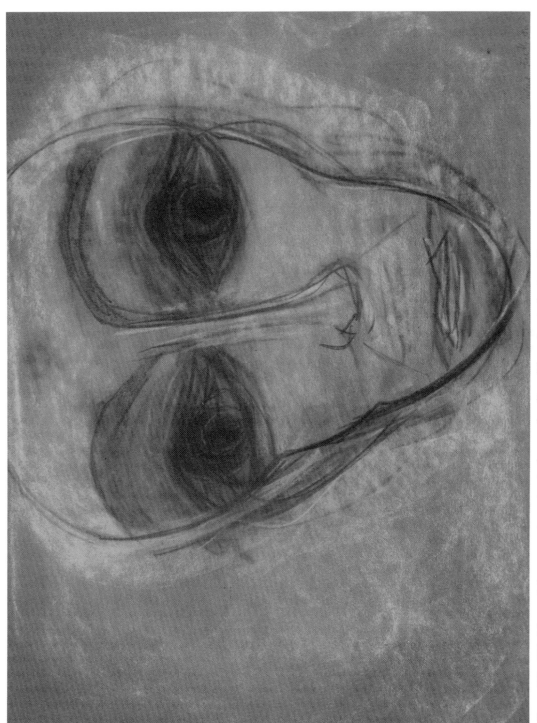

Illus. 29. "Cold and hunger penetrated our bodies like sharp knives."

Illus. 30. "I vowed that we would not become dead souls."

Where was she? I could not leave without her. We were losing our one chance to escape from Auschwitz. Frantically, I searched for her among the masses of shaved heads, naked, stumbling bodies (Illus. 31). Then I saw her and fought my way toward her and gripped her firmly. We surged toward the cattle car. Hands reached out to us. Our group pulled us into the open car. We had barely made it. Minutes later, the doors slammed shut.

Illus. 31. "Frantically, I searched for her . . ."

It had taken us three days to reach hell, and it took us the same number of days to leave it. We arrived at Unterluss, a small industrial town about thirty kilometers from Bergen-Belsen (Illus. 32).

A small work camp on its outskirts was our final destination. I was assigned the night shift—8:00 P.M. to 4:00 A.M. I cleaned schrapnel at the I.G. Farben factory. The nights were bitterly cold and we had to walk ten kilometers to and from camp. I barely kept my eyes open during my shift. But I had to stay awake: the SS aroused sleepers by prodding them with their rifle butts. I managed, therefore, not to drift off.

Illus. 32. "We arrived at Unterluss . . ."

I remember one SS officer with particular clarity. She was second-in-command of our camp. We called her the "brown one," and even the guards feared her (Illus. 33). Astride her horse, she looked down on us with strangely piercing eyes. Once during rollcall, she whipped a friend of mine, a very pretty girl who worked in the office. After the beating my friend was unable to move for days.

Illus. 33. "We called her the 'brown one.'"

After two months, they assigned me to a construction gang dipping a foundation for a building. The work was hard, especially in our weakened state (Illus. 34). Nevertheless, it was better than any death camp (Illus. 35). After a while, because I was a good worker, they made me a foreman. From then on, life was a little easier. (Mother had been lucky enough to draw kitchen detail.) We even began to hope. Above our heads, came the roar of American planes. In the woods, we spotted the tinfoil that they dropped. Like overwound clocks, we began to wait for liberation.

Illus. 34. "The work was hard, especially in our weakened state."

Illus. 35. "It was better than a death camp."

April 12, 1945. Light woke us up. It was impossible that they had let us oversleep. Yet, here we were still in our barracks. Where were the guards? Suddenly, we realized—the SS were gone.

In those first moments of freedom some women ran into the woods. Most of us raced instead to the kitchen looking for food. One barrel of yellow colored jam remained. We took turns eating it, smearing our lips with the gooey stuff. We looked at each other. Dazed, we were all quite dazed (Illus. 36).

Illus. 36. "Dazed, we were all quite dazed."

Our freedom was short-lived. Three hours later trucks arrived carrying armed civilians. They took us to Bergen-Belsen (Illus. 37). It was too much—from hope to this. Corpses lay piled up like garbage (Illus. 38). We could barely distinguish the few survivors from their dead companions. The living were naked, covered with lice. Next to them we looked like superwomen. At least flesh lightly coated our bones. (I weighed about 100 pounds.) Already too my hair had begun to grow back. I had only to shake it and it curled. We were even clothed in human garb, our striped blue and gray work camp uniforms.

Illus. 37. "They took us to Bergen-Belsen."

Illus. 38. "Corpses lay piled up like garbage."

We first responded to Bergen-Belsen with shock. A curious guilt assailed us too (Illus. 39). We had had the easier time. Enduring Auschwitz, we had thought we had lived through hell, but a facade of humanity, the geraniums and the bathhouses, the watery soup and the tough slabs of bread had existed. In Auschwitz we saw smoke but not bodies. There, only suicides died visibly (Illus. 40).

Illus. 39. "A curious guilt assailed us."

Of course, we knew that our not seeing was calculated, that the truth had to be hidden because it was too awful, that the camouflage represented another form of contempt. Yet it saved us too. It told us that our tormentors still recognized us as humans capable of being deceived, and capable too of maintaining a vestige of dignity.

Here in Bergen-Belsen the last facade had been stripped away. The stench of all those decayed and decaying bodies clung to our skin, filled our nostrils, made our eyes water with tears. Within hours lice covered us also. Mother tried to pick them out of my hair, but it was futile.

Three days later the British Army liberated us. When we saw the first soldiers, mother and I broke down and cried (Illus. 41). Our rescuers fed us green pea soup with fatty meat until we could eat no more. A day or two later I watched as our former captors, obeying orders, began to pile the dead bodies into trucks.

Some of the women surrounded the trucks yelling and throwing rocks at them. I was too exhausted to join in. I came down with diphtheria. I could not stop choking and hovered close to death. The Red Cross hadn't arrived yet but a fellow prisoner gave me an injection of I don't know what. Whatever it was, it saved my life.

Shortly thereafter we were transferred to a different barrack. For many it was already too late. Of the original 800, 200 died, among them my aunt. Everyone in our group contracted typhoid. In addition I had yellow jaundice. Mother had developed a thrombosis.

Illus. 41. "Mother and I broke down and cried."

Several weeks later I regained some of my strength and felt energetic enough to nurse mother. One time I ventured into town with a British soldier in a jeep. A German family provided some necessities including soap and a dozen eggs.

For the first time I began to dream of going home, finding our loved ones and telling our story. But mother was not well enough to go on an uncertain journey. By August, however, the situation had improved enough for me to make arrangements with the Red Cross for our transportation to Sweden.

On our arrival in Malmo, mother was moved immediately to a sanitorium, and I was placed in quarantine. For an eternity it seemed, I didn't know exactly where she was, or whether she still lived. At the time, a terrific state of disorganization existed. But not for nothing had I exerted all my efforts in camp to save my mother. I was determined now to find her and made such a nuisance of myself that eventually they located the nursing home to which she had been sent.

My quarantine in Malmo ended in September. I was taken to Goteborg; mother was in a nursing home nearby, and later we were reunited. Around October news reached us that father was alive and living in a town near Prague. We received a telegram from our New York cousins. They had found our names on the list of survivors prepared by the Red Cross. The telegram informed us of father's whereabouts. Also, after our release I had sent a letter home saying we were safe in Sweden. The letter had reached Munkacs, were my father had read it. After he had been freed, he had returned home, only to be thrown out by the Russians, who, in addition, had confiscated his property. Like the adjacent areas, Munkacs was incorporated into the USSR. With Moricz father had then journeyed on to Prague.

The four of us were soon reunited. (Moricz had earlier linked up with father.) For two years we stayed in an apartment in Usti Nad/Labem, a town near the Elbe River, two hours by train from Prague. Again, we waited, but it was a different kind of waiting. This time we waited to immigrate to the United States.

Meanwhile, I took a course in cosmetics, had the tooth fixed that the SS guard broke, learned Czech, and accompanied father on his numerous trips to see about immigration. Looking around me, I saw that, while outwardly, I resembled other women my age who had survived, I was somehow different. Because their parents had perished, they wanted to marry and have children. Because my parents had survived, I wanted to look after them. The habits I had learned so painfully in the death camps lingered. At last in February 1948, our immigration papers came through.

So our little family arrived in New York. I was the first to get a job. I worked in a beauty shop in Manhattan. After my third paycheck I bought my first piece of American clothing: a short coat then fashionable called a "topper." Three months later I met my future husband. He had returned two years before, after serving in the United States Army. There was an immediate link between us: his parents had been in Auschwitz, where they had died. In February 1949, we married. Within a year I became a U.S. citizen.

* * *

I take up my brush and dab some green on the canvas. The patch of color grows larger and rounder. Round as the moon. Round as the cabbages of Auschwitz (Illus. 42). And once again, I am lying between rows of cabbages, the moon shining in that dark Polish sky, the earth damp beneath my body. It reads like some gruesome

Illus. 42. "Round as the moon. Round as the cabbages in Auschwitz."

fairy tale by the Brothers Grimm. One day the princess died and was resurrected the same night in a cabbage field. Although she lived happily afterwards, she could never be like other people. She is marked by a crimson X that turns green, an indelible mark (Illus. 43 and 44). No matter how much she enjoys life, the mark reminds

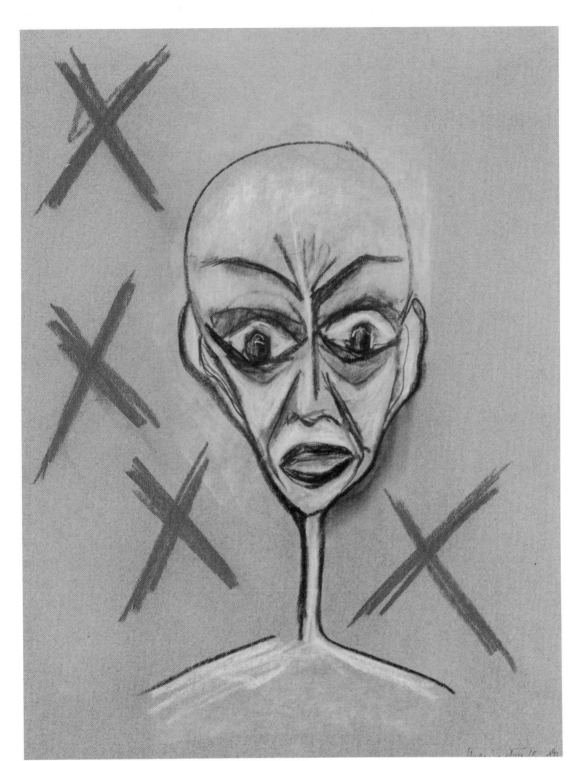

Illus. 43. "She is marked by a crimson X."

Illus. 44. ". . . an indelible mark."

her of her life-in-death, and a voice inside whispers again, "You're not like others." And the same voice, deepening with anger, asks God, "Why me?" (Illus. 45)

Illus. 45. "Why me?"

Afterword

FOR ME REMEMBERING THE HOLOCAUST is only recent. About eight years ago I passed through a personal crisis. As one does during such periods, I examined my life closely. Up to then I thought that I had succeeded quite well in living in the present. As I looked more closely, however, I realized that in many ways, like roots spreading thickly underground, my experiences of that time had affected my life profoundly. They had, in effect, shaped me into the woman I am today.

From one of my art teachers I learned that "Art exists in order to embody eternal values." I believe this to be so. What messages, then, do the faces of those who have survived and the faces of those who have perished have to transmit, the faces that haunt me—of the old men and the young, of girls just emerging into womanhood, boys with new hair above their lips, the too pale faces of children? That is for you to decide. For my part, I know that any survivor attempting to communicate with himself or with others via speech, the written word, or the visual arts must admit the inadequacy of even these means in relating its horrors. Yet with the optimism chiseled in Auschwitz, I hope to reach the generations to come so that they will never let it happen again.

I also hope to communicate a nightmare world where human beings were subjected to a profound and systematic assault on the very core of self. I am still amazed that, in the midst of this hell, so many found ways to assert their own moral dignity. Once released, we found our job undone, for now we had to recharge, to build new lives despite our tattered souls. So once again we started, somehow gathering the energy and optimism to give birth to a new generation that would begin to replace the one and one-half million murdered children.

These paintings and sculptures are only fragments—splinters, really—of the six million pictures that reside in my head. As I work on them, we engage in conversation of the best kind. They are my teachers, speaking to me in low, persistent voices about the great paradoxes of life in death and death in life. Finally, they make me humble before the gifts given to me—an ability for artistic expression, life, and, perhaps most important, the capacity for love (Illus. 46–60).

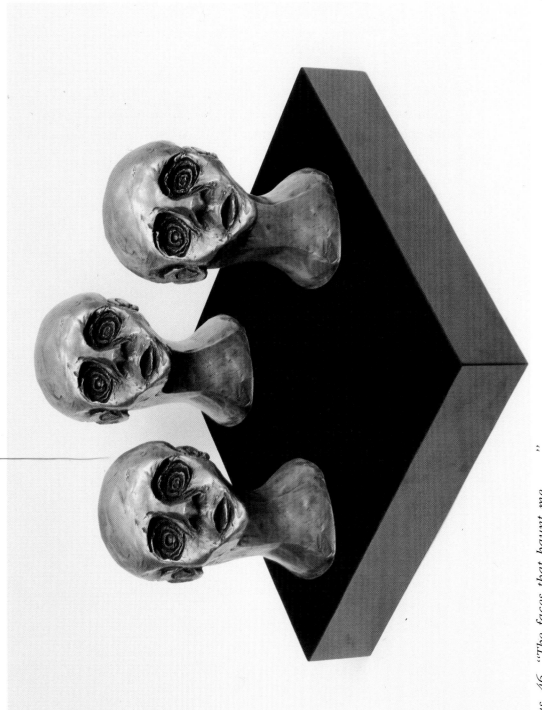

Illus. 46. "The faces that haunt me. . . ."

Illus. 47. ". . . of the old men and the young. . . ."

Illus. 48. "... girls just emerging into womanhood. ..."

Illus. 49. "The inadequacy of art to reveal its horrors . . ."

Illus. 50. "the nightmare world that seeps into our dreams. . . ."

Illus. 51. "We recharged. . . ."

*Illus. 52. ". . . picked ourselves up and
began anew. . . ."*

Illus. 53. "So once again we started. . . ."

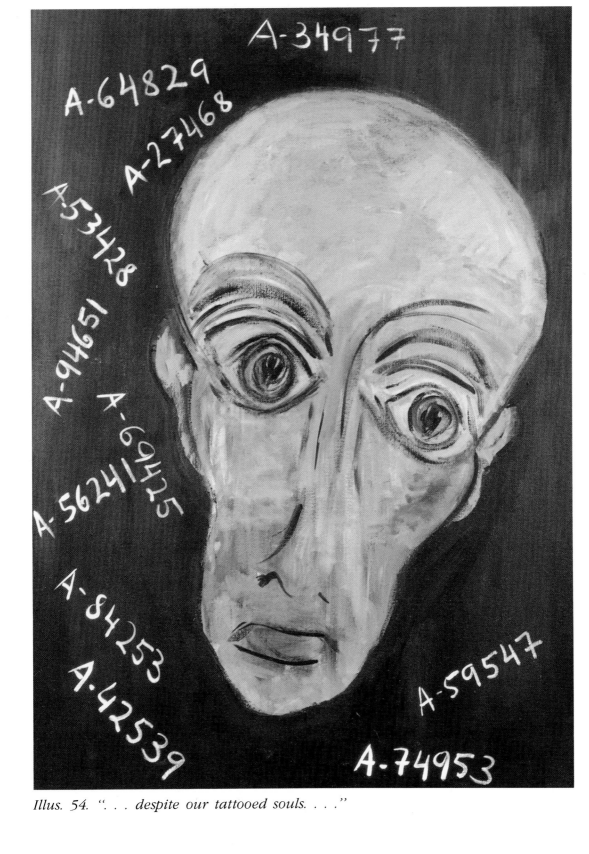

Illus. 54. ". . . despite our tattooed souls. . . ."

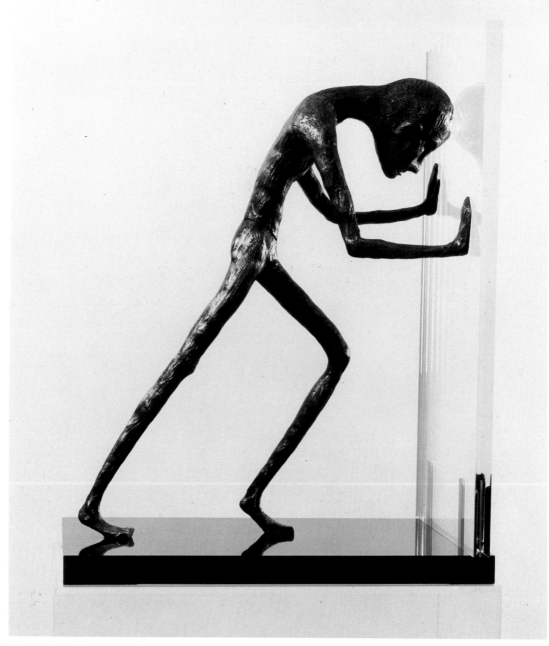

Illus. 55. "Despite the obstacles we had to face. . . ."

Illus. 56. ". . . and gave birth to a new generation. . . ."

Illus. 57. ". . . to replace . . . the one and one half million children who had died."

Illus. 58. "The paintings and sculptures are only fragments."

Illus. 59. "We speak together about life in death. . . ."

Illus. 60. ". . . and death in life."

1988

THIS YEAR I returned to Auschwitz. However, now I stayed only six hours, on a cold and dreary March afternoon. I came with sixteen other people, including my husband, who were part of a tour sponsored by the Simon Wiesenthal Center. The tour is a yearly affair, and the center tries on each trip to take at least one survivor of the death camps. Of our group, I was that survivor.

Why had I decided to return? In the months after I finally told the center to include us on the trip, this question flitted in and out of my head. I answered it by saying that my art was at a standstill: on the one hand, when I painted the Holocaust, something was missing. On the other hand, when I tried to escape from my experience, I made pretty pictures. Neither was an acceptable possibility. Perhaps I needed to rekindle my anger at what had happened to me and those I had loved at Auschwitz and the other camps. Lately, I had felt it diminishing, and though in one way this was good, I also felt that there were still too many blanks in my memory. If I were really to come to terms with Auschwitz, then I needed to confront it again.

These were the reasons I gave myself for going in the months before our departure, when I thought at all about what I had embarked on. Most of the time, however, life flowed on comfortably, and what awaited me seemed far away.

On the one-hour bus trip from Cracow to Auschwitz, my feelings changed. I had been asked by Rhonda, the director of the Wiesenthal Center in New York, who accompanied us, to say a few words. Back in the hotel, the speech I had prepared seemed quite satisfactory, but now on the bus I had difficulty speaking because, as we sped through the countryside, pictures of camp life began, like photographs in a darkroom, to enlarge in my mind. And as they succeeded one another in a silent progression, I wanted desperately to feel what I had felt when I first passed through the gates of Auschwitz—as I stood waiting on endless lines to use the latrines, as I lay huddled on my bunk in Barrack C. So, instead of my prepared speech, I said a few words and sat down.

We passed through the gate. Had there been brick buildings in that Auschwitz? All the structures I remembered had been of wood. No, this is not where I had lived and most of my family had died. But there was the crematorium chimney, the look-out towers (but hadn't they been wooden too?), and the barbed wire. Where was I? Meanwhile, the young Polish woman who was our guide had joined us and began talking. She was cool, detached, brisk, and I disliked her immediately. Her voice and manner grated on me. How dare she talk statistics; it was my brother, my nephews, my aunts she was reducing to numbers. (On the night before, I had counted up thirty-six members of my immediate family who had died in the camps.) Impatiently, I broke into the guide's patter.

"Where was C Camp, Barracks 26?" I asked. Her smooth progression interrupted, she became annoyed.

"Camp C was in Birkenau. We'll go there after the museum."

Two other groups were in the dark cool museum with us: a crowd of German tourists and some Hasidim from Israel. A map showed three camps. It was then I recalled that where we had just entered was not the place where I and my family had arrived. The site of the museum had originally housed political prisoners. Until this moment, I had never realized that Camp C, Barracks 26 had been a part of Birkenau.

I asked our guide where the kitchen was on the map. She showed it to me. When I said that I would like to see it, she answered that we would go there after the museum. I had seen many of the pictures on the walls of the museum, but was unprepared for the rush of emotion I felt on looking at the glass cases filled with human hair, toothbrushes, shoes, and suitcases of the camp's inmates. My Aunt Ida's hair, my cousin Nellie's toothbrush, the hiking shoes I had worn at arrival, the backpack my mother carried with her to camp. . . . Were they somewhere in these desolate piles of human debris?

Our last stop in the museum was the small room of eternal light. As I knelt down and lit candles, their flames came up and with them, my life in the Auschwitz inferno rose up too, the flames licking but not burning the images of lost ones from my mind. I felt my husband's hand on my shoulder. Deeply affected, he too was mourning the death of loved ones—the father and step-mother who had vanished in the Nazi night.

After the museum, we got on the bus for our ride to Birkenau. Once again, we entered through an iron gate, but this time I knew where I was. A field, wooden barracks, a brick chimney told me that, after nearly forty years, I had found the way back to my Auschwitz.

Again, I asked the guide, "Where is the kitchen? Where is Camp C?"

She replied that nothing remained of Camp C except some brick chimneys.

"Can we go there anyway?"

"Impossible, the gates are locked. We can, however, see the ruins of the crematorium."

Nothing to be done. As we approached the ruins, the forest, used by the Nazis as a holding place when the crematorium was too full, loomed menacingly (Illus. 61). Nearby, I glimpsed a lake, the same lake into which the ashes of the dead had been dumped. But it was Camp C, not them, that holds my attention. I try to zoom in on it with my cam camera.

"Can we go to the barracks in Camp A?" I ask, already anticipating the No that is the answer.

"We don't have time," the guide says. But, after I tell Rhonda I am not leaving until we stand on that ground, and she had a whispered conversation with the guide, it is decided that we will see the barracks after all.

It is not Barracks 26, Camp C, but all the barracks were identical in their arrangement and structure, so I will have to be content, and as I stand on the barracks floor, for the first time since we arrived I am no longer a tourist. I am cold and hungry; my mother is talking to me with a worried look on her face about food, recipes. She is praying, she is crying, "Where are my sisters, my brothers?" Beside her, I am vowing, "I won't die, and I won't let her die."

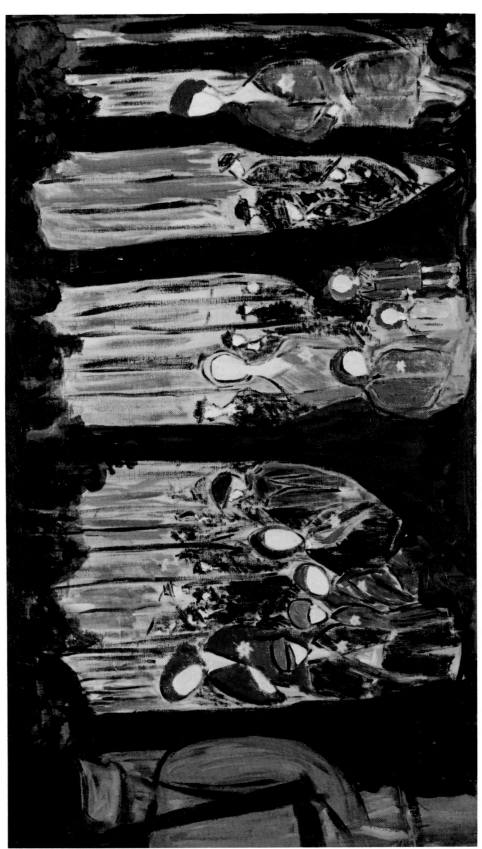

Illus. 61. ". . . the forest used by the Nazis as a holding place."

I came back to reality. Now I know why I have returned to Auschwitz: to make sure that what happened to me forty years ago was not a dream, to renew the pledge I made in my art: to grip those who see my work so that they will remember what happened to us and never let it happen again. I look around me at the wooden slats that once held my shivering body. I am ready to leave.

But that night in the hotel room, my head spins with images. One that recurs is of the ditch where I used to get water to wash after it had rained. There had been a rag. How had I ever acquired it? My possessions had been reduced to zero. This small rag was half the size of a handkerchief. I had used it as my washcloth, towel and pillow case.

Theresienstadt, which we visited three days later, looked civil in contrast to Auschwitz. The sky was blue, and we had a new guide— a middle-aged Czech with a human face. Though we were never shown the part of the camp where the Jews were housed, I was not so angry as I had been with the Polish accountant. By the fake cemetery which the Nazis had built to hide the fact that no bodies slept underneath the headstones—for all that remained of these dead were their ashes—we read aloud poems written by the children of Theresienstadt. In this peaceful setting of death, their clear voices, alive to the world's beauty, were unbearably moving.

It is almost a month since I have returned home. Since then, I have wakened each morning with a great heaviness in my body. One day I identify this feeling: It is how I used to feel lying pressed against my mother on the wooden slats that were our beds in Auschwitz.

I have returned home. Patiently, I wait to see how my art will contain the answers to the questions that set me forth on this painful journey back.